Fart Club

Fart Club

**A guide to maximizing your meager potential
through your dirty stink hole**

Angus Beeftickle MD

ISBN: 0692540873
ISBN 13: 9780692540879

To my beautiful wife and two beautiful daughters
I love you dearly. You remind me daily how blessed I
am.

To my mom, my dad, and my brother
Your unconditional love and consistent support are the
foundation on which I have built my life.

To Brian, Levy, Mike, and Pat
Your input and suggestions have been invaluable.
Without your help, I doubt this book would have ever
been finished.

Thank you all.

INTRODUCTION

M̲ake no mistake, my friend. There is a war out there—
a war against flatulence. Through history, flatulence
has been scorned in polite company. Thought to be vile
and crude, people were encouraged to repress this natural
bodily function. Because of this attitude, gas has been forced
into the shadows. Even in public bathrooms, most indi-
viduals demonstrate a certain uneasiness during its release.
Unfortunately, most of society has bought into this dogmatic
existence. I have termed this way of life Colonic Restraint.

During my adolescence I too fell prey to the repression
that is Colonic Restraint. It was not until my young-adult
years when I realized something was very wrong. I began to
question convention and thus began a quest of self-discovery. Rumblings deep in my gut kept pushing me onward—
but toward what?

For some reason, god has blessed me with the ability
to produce prolific amounts of gas. This has forced me to

become better than most at controlling my abdominal muscles and anal sphincter. Over the years I developed unique and varied ways in which to release this natural resource.

I pay attention to the details. Small nuances in pitch and length can make all the difference. Initially this was for my own enjoyment, with an occasional show for close friends and anyone who happened to be at the next urinal. Slowly, however, something amazing began to happen. My fear of embarrassment no longer held sway over me. Soon a well-timed rip in a movie theater became commonplace. The gloves, so to speak, were off, and the opportunities were limitless.

There are others, like myself, who have also broken the shackles of Colonic Restraint. We form an undercurrent of rebellion—a sort of counterculture, if you will. This shared experience has bonded us like brothers, giving us strength and courage to continue to fight the good fight. This is a struggle to change the hearts and minds of the masses—to encourage people's own self-discovery and to eradicate the stigma and embarrassment associated with farting in public.

I now offer you one of my favorite speeches from *A Few Good Men*, slightly altered for my own nefarious purposes.

> We live in a world with walls, and those walls have
> to be guarded by men with gas. Who's going to do

it—you? I have a greater responsibility than you can possibly fathom. You reward Colonic Restraint, and you curse the shart. You have that luxury. You have the luxury of not knowing what I know. That sharting, while tragic, makes people laugh. Its existence, while grotesque and incomprehensible to you, is funny. You don't want the truth, because, deep down, in places you don't talk about at parties, you want me on that wall. You need me on that wall. We use phrases like "ass-belch," "the brown noise," and "dirty bomb." We use these phrases as the backbone of a life spent defending something. You use them as a punch line. I have neither the time nor the inclination to explain myself to a man who privately chuckles in response to the blanket of rectal fog I provide and then publicly questions the manner in which I provide it. I would rather you had just said thank you and went on your way. Otherwise I suggest you load up on cabbage stew and stand a post.

A *shart* (a.k.a. an inconvenient deuce) is an unfortunate situation whereby one soils oneself during the forceful expulsion of a fart.

❖ ❖ ❖

CHAPTER I

CRUDE BEGINNINGS

M y story begins in rural northern Michigan. The kind of place where people don't lock their doors. Where parents teach their kids right from wrong. Where good, God-fearing people go to church on Sunday.

I had two great parents, and I have no complaints about my childhood. I was just like any other kid until about the age of 8. It was at this time I began to realize I was different. It seemed no matter what I did, my gas was terrible. My mother would get mad at me and make me go to the bathroom, even when I didn't have to go. This had little effect on my self-esteem, as I found my farts funny. (How little things have changed). I got a kick out of people's reactions. The gas attacks continued despite my mother's best efforts. I guess, in this case, nature beat nurture.

Once I entered middle school, things started to change. I realized that girls generally didn't like guys who smelled bad. So peer pressure forced me to put a lid on it, so to speak.

I continued with the status quo until one fateful night in January 1991. I was in the tenth grade and had to attend a city counsel meeting for a social studies class. This meeting was in an old courtroom filled with wooden benches, like the kind you would find in a church. As usual I was gassy. I had been holding back for quite some time, as my girlfriend was with me. I needed to release some of the pressure but didn't want to disturb the meeting by getting up to go to the bathroom. I decided to take care of things right there. What should have been a routine, *silent* slider turned into a disaster. Just as soon as I leaned over to my left cheek, two hours worth of gas was released without prejudice. Everybody in the courtroom could easily hear the reverberation off the wooden bench. It was a stunning turn of events—a rookie mistake, usually made by lesser men.

I stared at the floor, paralyzed with shame. I could not bear to face those around me. A funny thing happened, though. I heard the most wonderful sound coming in from all angles. It was laughter. As I slowly looked up, I witnessed multitudes of people in the grips of laughter: the kind of laughter that makes little sound but causes your shoulders to shake—the kind of laughter that's hard to repress in such a sterile environment. I don't even think anyone was upset by my courtroom outburst, save for one old man sitting next to me. The laughter swept over me as well and basically continued intermittently until the meeting was adjourned one hour later.

This experience affected me greatly. My mother had always taught me that farting in public was unacceptable. I had taken her words at face value and never questioned them. But there I was, farting in a serious public forum, and nothing bad happened. Not only that, but people actually found humor in the situation. How could this be?

I had to see if that night was just a fluke, so I started an informal investigation. Later that year, I blasted a huge fart in homeroom. It was even louder than my courtroom rip. The other students lost it. Even the teacher had a hard time composing himself. Again, no punishment or retribution was handed down. The only result, as far as I could see, was uncontrollable laughter.

So began my great social experiment. The shenanigans continued through high school and into college. While at college I met others who were like me: people who were not afraid to push the boundaries of social acceptance. Our small co-op began to multiply. Soon we were pushing one another to take it to the next level. After a while nothing was off limits. The library became our proving ground.

While studying we would position ourselves in strategic locations to disrupt the maximum number of people. Most of the time, the patrons found the outbursts funny and welcomed the lighthearted study break. Once in a while, though, people took great offense to the whole affair. Their verbal lashings only added to our enjoyment of the experience.

After college I met a girl (my future wife) through a dating service. Yes, a dating service. We hit it off quite well, and after several dates I was invited to spend the night at her place. This was still a critical time in the courtship: a time when both of us were still trying hard to impress the other, and when neither one had enough information to make a final judgment. One wrong move could send this romantic house of cards crashing down.

That night, my daughter was conceived. No, just kidding. Things did go rather well, though. The following morning we were spooning. I was in front, and she in back. I was in a semiconscious state and had momentarily forgot that I was in somebody else's bed. I had a large bubble of gas in my gut, and I instinctively pushed.

I have to say that the length and volume was quite startling. The sheer force of the fart woke me out of my blissful ignorance into a world of profound embarrassment and dread. I just lay there, silently praying to baby Jesus that she didn't wake up. As I lay there contemplating my next move, my girlfriend started to laugh. Her laughter caused me to laugh, so she knew I was awake. I laughed it off, pretending to have done it on purpose—like this somehow made my farting more acceptable. I thought, in my panic, such a ridiculous ploy would make me appear supremely self-confident—like James Bond meets the Marquis de Sade.

Well, she must not have been all that bothered by "the incident" as we are still married. In the end, it was actually beneficial as it set the tone for our relationship moving forward. This is yet another example of farting in front of others without any negative consequences.

You might think, after all this, I would have become rather calloused about farting in front of others. Some would even use the word "insensitive." I see it differently. I am quite sensitive about people's reactions, as this is the whole point. I use gas as a tool to provoke emotion in others—much like an artist uses paint.

My challenge to you now is to experience this social rebellion for yourself. Share your experiences with others, and encourage them to join the resistance. Shed the shackles of Colonic Restraint, and thou shalt truly be free. I realize not everyone is ready to take on this challenge. However, if you feel moved by my words, then I encourage you to continue on to the next chapter. I will be there, waiting.

❖ ❖ ❖

CHAPTER II

KNOWLEDGE IS POWER

As with any good revolution, knowledge is power. Historically, those who posses it have the power. They understand an uneducated populace is easily manipulated and can be bent to their will. Enlighten the masses, however, and you galvanize them into a plunger of change when things become stagnant. My goal with this book is to equip all who read with the necessary information and techniques to become that plunger. The journey is not easy. You will be asked to surrender your preconceived notions and your ego at the door. You will need to be disciplined in regard to the content and timing of your meals. Most importantly, you will need to be courageous in your execution of duty. Complete this journey, however, and you will become a foghorn of social change.

I have completed my own journey of discovery and now feel ready to guide others down this difficult path. First, though, let me make something crystal clear. I am not your friend. We are not pals or amigos. You are not going to get your gear and bunk up with me. Rather, I will be your tormentor for the remainder of this book, like the mosquito in a dark room: always there, but just out of reach. I am here to break you down and build you back up again in my likeness. I will never quit on you, even though you will want to quit on yourself. I am the alpha and the omega; I am the creator and destroyer. With God as my witness, you will rise like a phoenix from the ashes of what once was your worthless existence.

As you read this book, you will find yourself wondering, "What man is this who does such things, and on whose authority does he speak?" My identity is not important. I am merely a conduit. At this point, you have done nothing to prove you are worthy of knowing me. You are a rock in my shoe. Besides, you have more pressing questions at hand— such as "How am I ever going to get laid looking like I do?"

Now that each player knows his or her part, we may proceed. There exist three levels of knowledge. Chapter III involves understanding the biochemical mechanisms of gas production. We build on this knowledge to master production. Chapter IV is where you will learn the art of distribution. In chapter V, you will be given access to multiple "fart recipes" you can use to customize your gas.   We will put it all together in chapter VI: "Commitment." You will not be permitted to proceed to a higher level until *mastery* of your current level is demonstrated. Passing for social reasons is unacceptable, even if you bring a note from your mother.

❖ ❖ ❖

CHAPTER III

UNDERSTANDING GAS PRODUCTION

A sad little man named Magenda first formally studied flatulence in 1816. His initial work identified methane and carbon dioxide as the two main components of flatus. I doubt if this man was ever married.

Since then many scientists have advanced our knowledge on the subject of gas. The major constituents of intestinal gas are now known to be nitrogen, hydrogen, carbon dioxide, methane, and oxygen [1]. Interestingly, these gasses are odorless but contribute greatly to a fart's "bark." The "bite" is due to thousands of tiny shit particles that are small enough to fit through the fibers of your jeans and aerosolize into the surrounding air. OK, not really. A fart's smell actually originates from trace amounts of highly odiferous, gaseous compounds. These include skatole, indole, hydrogen sulfide, volatile amines, and short-chain fatty acids. Pay attention, numbnuts.

The overall composition of intestinal gas is influenced by both intrinsic and extrinsic factors. Age, diet, ethnicity, colonic bacterial colonization, altitude, and the extent of air swallowing (linked to gum-chewing and ill-fitting dentures) all contribute to its volume and character.

TIP: Don't get bullied into a fart contest against a gum-chewing elderly man with dentures who lives in the Alps and makes his own sauerkraut. You will likely lose.

Chronologically and genetically speaking, you play the hand you're dealt. Where we can effect change is through the diet. (Although air swallowing is a plus.) On an *average* diet, the healthy knucklehead reading this book will produce 60–70 ml of gas per hour [1]. That amounts to almost one half gallon of shit particles per day. In one year, that is equal to nearly 150 gallons! That is enough to fill at least thirty monkey-sized space suits. With some small changes in diet, you will easily be able to quadruple that number.

Excessive flatus has been reported to follow the inclusion in the diet of a variety of foods. Table 1 lists the top thirty gas-producing foods.

Table 1

Apples	Apricots	Artichokes
Asparagus	Bananas	Beans
Broccoli	Brussels sprouts	Cabbage
Carrots	Cauliflower	Cheese
Corn	Fruit drinks	Ice cream
Milk/milk products	Nuts	Oat bran
Onions	Pasta	Peaches
Pears	Peas	Potatoes
Prunes	Raisins	Seeds
Soft drinks	Spinach	Whole wheat

Learn them, love them, live them. No excuses, asshole. Commit them to memory, because these foods are going to be your greatest ally. When in doubt—when in need—go to them, for they will be as comforting as a back-cracking bear hug from an old friend.

So what is it about some foods that make them better gas-producers than others? In a nutshell, it's sugar. Oligosaccharides, to be exact. This is a big name for a small molecule. Humans lack the enzyme necessary to break this type of sugar down. We rely on the bacteria that colonize our large intestine for this dirty little task. They are able to "digest" oligosaccharides, and the major by-product is carbon dioxide. This is a similar reaction used to carbonate beer. It's like having your own mobile brewery. Bottoms up!

Many of the foods on this list have an assortment of oligosaccharides, which contribute to their potency. Beans in particular have a large amount of sugar as well as fiber. This combo further increases their flatulence factor. Soaking or boiling beans prior to cooking may decrease up to 60 percent of their oligosaccharide content. Don't do that.

Fats also play an important role in gas production. The addition of fat to any meal will slow the gut's motility. This means food takes longer to come out from below, hence further increasing gas production and bloating. Who's the big winner? You're the big winner.

TIP: Why do some turds float, while others take their rightful place at the bottom of the bowel? Trapped and absorbed gas within the dirty thing give it buoyancy, causing it to float. It may also have something to do with its fat content. I'm not really sure, to be honest. Look, I'm no expert on fecal buoyancy. I'm just throwing ideas out there.

This next table (table 2) is from a study by Murphy et al. published in 1972 [2]. Before we review this information, I feel it is important that you understand just what lengths researchers have gone to obtain this type of data. For your edification (and amusement), I have included a passage from one such experiment by J. Tomlin and friends [3].

"The collections began between 0900 and 1300, after the volunteers had opened their bowels. Flatus gas was collected by means of a flexible gas impermeable rubber tube, the tip of which was inserted 40 mm into the anus and held in place with either surgical tape or the subject's underclothes. The other end of the tube was attached to one of the arms of a plastic T-connector, which was in turn connected to a laminated gas bag that was impermeable to gas diffusion. The competence of this gas-collection system was validated in two volunteers who submerged the lower parts of their bodies into warm water for one hour, during which time there were no detectable leaks (bubbling), and gas was collected in the bags".

The authors go on to describe the protocol volunteers are to follow when they need to move their bowels.

"If they experienced a need to defecate they were instructed to close off the current gas bag, remove the tube from the anus, defecate, clean the tip of the tube if necessary with a cotton bud, reinsert the tube, and attach a new bag as quickly as possible".

I am both appalled and impressed when reading papers such as these. How, by the beard of Zeus, did these scientists convince some sorry sumbitch to do these things to himself? To add insult to injury, the information obtained from said experiment is not particularly useful. I mean, it doesn't exactly advance man's standing in the universe. If I possessed such powers of persuasion, I would rule the world by now. OK, enough about that. Go ahead and look at the table now.

Table 2

Food ingredient	Intake (g)	Flatus (ml/h)	Food ingredient	Intake (g)	Flatus (ml/h)
Full-fat soya	146	30	California white beans	450	36
Soybeans	100	36	Lima beans	100	42
Soybeans	200	24	Mung beans	100	25
Defatted soya	146	71	Dutch brown beans	250	72
Soya grits	136	32	Dutch brown beans	175	51
Navy bean meal	146	179	Dutch brown beans	160	40
Whole bengal gram	40	52	Dun peas	125	21
Bengal gram	40	44	Dun peas	210	43
Red gram	40	48	Dun peas	210	29
Green gram	40	30	Lentils	200	41
California white beans	100	120–137	Lentils	200	34
California white beans	100	37	Red kidney beans	100	84

I don't know what half the items on this list are. I show this table only to illustrate the point that not all beans are created equal. Pay particular attention to navy bean meal, California white beans, and red kidney beans. The addition of just one of this terrible trio can increase gas production five to sixfold. Enough said. Honorable mention goes to dutch brown beans, because I like saying "dutch brown beans."

Murphy and his merry band of social misfits went a step further, determining the timing of maximal flatus output. Pay attention, as this will become important in chapter IV: Distribution.

> "Following the consumption of a meal containing beans or bean extracts, a healthy subject produced no extra gas for the first three hours. (What did the unhealthy subjects do?). Thereafter the level increased to its peak at five hours and declined back to baseline within seven hours [2]."

The point is to enjoy a healthy bean-meal five hours before your next road trip or board meeting.

Various medical conditions can also have a profound effect on the nature and frequency of one's farts. It's what I like to call a fart's methane footprint. This includes anything that alters intestinal motility (the speed at which food travels though the gut), nutrient absorption, and intestinal flora (types of bacteria that colonize the intestine). Worldwide, the most common of these ailments is lactose intolerance. Those of you who suffer from lactose intolerance damn well know what I'm talking about. The cross you must bear is a result of a deficiency in an enzyme called lactase. Lactase is responsible for hydrolysis (breakdown) of lactose. Lactose is a type of sugar commonly found in dairy products. Are you still with me? Symptoms of bloating, abdominal pain, and diarrhea often follow ingestion of dairy products. This is a consequence of the fermentation of undigested lactose in the colon. We must endeavor to control this great natural resource. This is a system poised for greatness—like a wild stallion that must be broken, only later to become a champion racehorse. You must become the "Colon Whisperer". With the right combo of foods, we should be able to generate prolific amounts of gas without diarrhea rearing its ugly head. You, my most deadly of warriors, can skip to level VI. You have all the tools you need.

❖ ❖ ❖

CHAPTER IV

DISTRIBUTION

Journeyman comedians know that it takes practice to be funny. The same is true of farting. Like a good joke, comedic farting requires impeccable timing and cadence. Let one drag out too long, and you lose your audience. Jump too fast to the punch line, and the buildup is lost (not to mention your clean underwear). Randomly releasing large volumes of gas is unrefined and not as funny as it could be. Here I will teach techniques to master the art of timing and control.

Use what you have learned in chapter III to increase over-all volume of gas. For one week, divide each workday into two-hour time blocks with ten-minute breaks in between. During each two-hour stretch, resist the urge to let any gas out. Not even a little slider. Some days this will be easy, but other days it will not. At each break, go to the bathroom (or your friend's cubical) and "release the kraken". You may eventually need to increase the lockout time to three hours. The goal here is twofold. First, we want to train the rectum to accept a greater volume of gas. So, instead of having just one in the chamber, you will eventually have "seventeen shots to the dome". We are also strengthening our external anal sphincter, enabling greater control.

The next phase of training involves controlled release. Using the techniques described above, store up a sizable volume of gas. Release a small portion, and then tighten your sphincter to stop the flow. Keep repeating this process until all gas is released. You should be able to stop each fart five to ten times. This takes coordination and "touch." You don't want to push too hard, as too much gas will be released between breaks. Practice this, because others will find great humor in your ability to deliver large numbers of farts at will.

If laughter were our only goal, that would be the end of the story. When a fart is executed correctly, laughter soon gives way to much darker emotions such as anger, fear, and a deep sense of betrayal. Scientists have known for years that odors can evoke deep-seated emotional responses. Olfactory receptors in your nose are directly connected to the limbic system, the most primitive part of the brain thought to be the seat of emotion. By ensuring that your gas reaches the olfactory receptors in others, you can deepen their experience.

This leads us into distribution. In my opinion, the most rewarding aspect of farting *is* distribution. You have all probably heard the koan (a paradoxical anecdote or riddle) that asks, "If a tree falls in the woods and no one is there to hear it, did it make a sound?" This question can easily be applied to farting. You can have the worst-smelling gas the world has ever known but if no one else experiences it, nobody wins. You need a reliable, reproducible way to get the gas from your ass to the nostrils of your victim. Like milk from the teat or beer from the tap, farts are always better direct from the source.

Tip: Why do farts smell? So deaf people can enjoy them too.

Over the years I have perfected several surefire ways to accomplish this distribution goal. I like to call this first method "The Mad Hatter". Please refer to illustration number 1 as you review instructions. First you will need a hat. Any hat will do, but fitted baseball caps are preferable. (The "trucker hat" is a poor choice because of its porous design.) Upon sensing an impending fart, the professional discretely removes his hat from his head and buries it between his or her legs. This release should be silent, to avoid alerting the victim. Upon release, the professional should pause for a count of five to allow all available gas to collect inside the hat. Then, in one smooth motion, the hat is swung from the crotch to the face of the victim. The object is to completely cover the face of the victim with the dome of the hat. In this way the victim will be taken by surprise and instinctively inhale. There are few things in life more rewarding than a perfectly executed Mad Hatter.

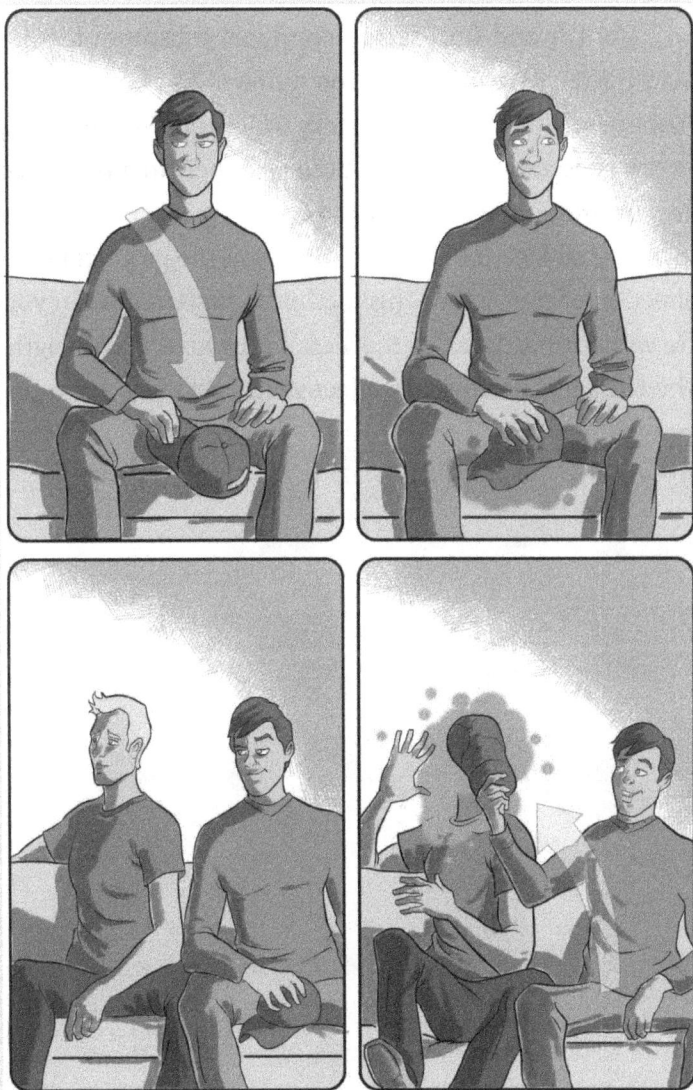

Illustration 1

"The Lift and Cut" is an acceptable substitute for the Mad Hatter. Refer to illustration number 2 as I read aloud. First, silently marinate your slacks while your unsuspecting victim goes about his or her business. Then, in a repetitive upward motion, use your hands to bring the product up toward your face. Inhale deeply and blow the product in the direction of the victim. This method is preferred when you are without headgear, or the victim is beyond arm's length. The Lift and Cut is usually effective for distances up to ten feet.

Illustration 2

The third and final distribution technique requires some athletic ability, flexibility, and complete disregard for discretion. I call it "The Cradle". Refer to illustration number 3 for details. First the professional must wait until maximum capacity has been reached in the rectal vault. The professional then suddenly leaps from his seat onto the floor. Care must be taken to avoid audible gas slippage, as this could be an embarrassing turn of events. The professional assumes an aggressive posture, with the back down and butt up in the air. Grasp behind each leg and pull back, bringing the giblets in close proximity to the face. The normal curvature of the sigmoid colon and rectum is straightened in this position, allowing great volumes of gas to pass in a short amount of time. With your lips tightened into a purse string, direct a fast-moving column of air over your bottom and directly at your victim. Properly executed, this method can be devastating.

Illustration 3

A fart's odor is much like the content of a joke. The truly funny ones are usually offensive. The odorless fart, on the other hand, can be a real letdown. It's like an empty promise. Not even ingenious methods of distribution can overcome the shortcomings of the "air biscuit". In inexperienced hands (and cheeks), it is little more than a roadside attraction—a tourist trap. Fear not, numbskulls, for I have the answer. I dub it "The Surprise". To pull off the Surprise, you need only the basics of timing and control. Bad odor, while always a plus, is not necessary. The Surprise goes like this: you come up with *any* excuse to have someone touch you in *any* capacity, and you fart at the very moment your victim touches you. It is just that simple. On first consideration, "The Surprise" may not seem all that amusing. Try it a few times, and see what happens. If you are creative, you can catch the same person over and over again. Therein lies the humor. Saying "Pull my finger" every time will not get it done. For example, if you have a growth on your arm, ask your wife, child, neighbor, or pastor to feel it. The moment they do, teach 'em a lesson. After several weeks ask the same person to feel the softness of your new shirt—and teach'em a lesson again. It is much like a game of chess: you have to be two to three moves ahead of your opponent. "The Surprise" is probably my personal favorite.

❖ ❖ ❖

CHAPTER V

RECIPES FOR DISASTER

To get your worthless bowels moving in the right direction, I will devote this entire chapter to fart recipes. These are just a few examples from my personal vault. I provide these as conversation pieces—icebreakers, if you will. This is by no means a complete list. Your challenge is to get out there and blaze your own path.

Just a quick note before getting started. In general, meals high in protein will result in low-volume, highly odiferous gas. Meals consisting of mostly carbs will result in high volume, pleasant-smelling gas. By adjusting the ratios of these foods, you can tailor your gas to meet any occasion.

Although results may vary, I have personally subjected myself to every one of these recipes and can vouch for their authenticity. Sixty percent of the time, they work every time.

EARTH, WIND, AND FIRE

3 parts nachos (with beef chili and jalapeños)
1 part wheat beer

Hot, earthy tones with a high grease factor. Jalapeños provide the fire upon release.

Moderate volume
Low potency
Moderate shart risk

MORNING GLORY

2 parts fried eggs
1 part orange juice
1 part corn beef hash

A distinct sulfur bouquet over an earthy background with plenty of volume.

High volume
Moderate potency
Moderate shart risk

THE TRUCKER

15 parts Vienna sausage
15 parts Wolf brand chili
15 parts strong coffee
1 part mild dehydration

Smells like a burning tire was put out with raw sewage—
simply put, the worst gas ever. Makes me angry just thinking
about it.

Low volume
Outrageous potency
Very high shart risk

THE EXCALIBUR

2 parts smoked turkey leg
4 goblets of flat beer
2 parts funnel cake with powdered sugar

Experience this medieval recipe after spending a day at your local renaissance festival eating carnival food and getting sunburnt. Reminiscent of unwashed peasant and campfire smoke. Comes standard with stomach ache. It's King Arthur's final revenge. Huzzah!

Low volume
Moderate potency
Moderate shart risk

BEEF WELLINGTON

2 parts beef tenderloin
1 part liver pâté
1 part egg
1 part pastry

This brings new meaning to Old English. Highly concentrated sulfur smell with heavy diesel overtones. It's what I imagine hell smells like.

Low volume
High potency
High shart risk

ICE-CREAM ANTISOCIAL

2 parts ice cream (any flavor)
1 part crushed peanuts
1 part lactose intolerance

I know grown men who have crapped themselves from lesser transgressions. Smells like a refrigerator full of food after a 7 day power outage.

High volume
High potency
Extremely high shart risk

BUFFALO BILL

2 parts bison burger
1 part cole slaw
1 part tall, light beer

Earthy, gamey, musk sent with a light sour finish. Overall dry.
Tends to produce a noise similar to kicking a flat soccer ball.

Low volume
Moderate potency
Low shart risk

TITILLATING TURKEY

4 parts turkey chili
2 parts corn bread
1 part sour cream
1 part diet cola

This one takes you by surprise with a heavy, sour, rotten-fruit overtone. I don't have a good explanation for it.

Moderate volume
Moderate potency
Low shart risk

THE ROSIE O'DONNELL

1 part navy beans
1 part brussels sprouts
1 part prune juice
1 part bacon

A nearly intolerable combination resulting in tons of hot air with little substance.

High volume
Low potency
Low shart risk

EL NIÑO

10 parts Corona with lime
4 parts "puffy" beef tacos
2 parts refried beans
2 parts tortilla chips

Plenty of volume. Smells like it came from some dark, recessed region of the colon that gets little or no blood supply.

Moderate volume
High potency
High shart risk

THE KAMIKAZE (A.K.A. DIVINE WIND)

6 parts California roll (sushi)
1 part soy sauce/ginger/wasabi
3 parts "sake-bomb"

Best described as moldy bread meets fresh trout. Odor is fairly intense.

Low volume
Moderate potency
Low shart risk

ITALIAN HEATBALLS

1 part ground beef
2 parts tomato-based spaghetti sauce
3 parts spaghetti
2 parts Cosmopolitan martini

Pungent, sour-diesel base with hints of dead rodent. Overall odor is quite bad, which is surprising because the meal is routine.

Moderate volume
Moderate potency
Low shart risk

YEAR OF THE SKUNK

3 parts hot and sour soup
2 parts garlic chicken with mushroom gravy over pan-fried noodles
2 parts chocolate malt

People will think a family of nervous skunks took up residence in your pants. Think this one through before you do it.

Moderate volume
High potency
Moderate shart risk

TIP: I have discovered that the addition of a malted milk shake after any meal will practically double the predicted gas volume.

GRAPES OF WRATH (A.K.A. SONOMA AROMA)

10 parts various wine samples
4 parts various cheese samples
2 parts tri-tip BBQ sandwich
1 part potato salad

Henry wouldn't be "Fonda" this one. Overpowering rotten-food smell with hints of grapefruit, pepper, oak, and chocolate. Surprising volume with a wet finish.

High volume
Moderate potency
High shart risk

SMOOTH CRIMINAL

15 parts Hometown Buffet
1 part coffee
1 part chocolate milk
1 part shared work space

The name says it all. This generic "fart smell" could easily be blamed on anybody. Silence is paramount, so don't get overly eager.

Moderate volume
Low potency
Moderate shart risk

Disclaimer: Odors vary depending on buffet items chosen.

LEUFTWAFFEN

3 parts wiener schnitzel
3 parts german potato salad
2 parts apple sauce
1 part spicy mustard
1 part Coke and Orange Fanta (Spezi)

You're sure to achieve air superiority against almost any foe with this one. Incredible volume with an odor reminiscent of garbage-truck juice.

High volume
Moderate potency
Low shart risk

THE WAWA

4–5 hours of binge drinking
4 parts nachos
2 parts Wawa processed cheese sauce
2 parts chopped Wawa hot dog
1 part Wawa refried beans
1 part canned jalepeños
1 part generic hot sauce

Primeval, disturbing, and anger-provoking—a scent normally found only at crime scenes. I can think of no other way to describe it. Bring extra underwear.

Moderate volume
High potency
Guaranteed shart

Warning: Will induce multiple bouts of loose stools.

STEWAGE

Rated a "Top Performer"
4 parts cabbage stew (with ham and potatoes)
2 parts watermelon wedges
1 part cold milk

You just can't go wrong with this one. Plenty of volume and longevity (over two hours of peak production) with a dry finish. Results are predictable and easily reproducible. Smells like cabbage turds.

High volume
Moderate potency
Low shart risk

TIP: Any cabbage dish will give similar results. I could write an entire chapter on cabbage dishes alone.

THE POWER LIFTER

4 parts high carbohydrate diet
2 parts "weight gainer" milk shake (milk + protein powder)
1 part raw aggression

Positively astounding volume with a mild pancake-batter scent. Causes "machine gun" farts while on treadmill.

Outrageous volume
Low potency
Low shart risk

THE MIRAGE (A.K.A. VEGAS TRASH)

20 parts alcohol
10 parts self-loathing
8 parts cigarettes
6 parts sleep deprivation
4 parts $50 room-service cheeseburger

From the feel and smell, you'll swear this one's wet. In reality, it's as hot and dry as the Nevada desert. Neglect your health in pursuit of empty promises for seventy-two straight hours, and this is what you get. Reminiscent of dirty diapers. Produces sickeningly sweet odor when combined with too much cologne.

Low volume
Moderate potency
Low shart risk

HOT CARL

4 parts Carl's Jr. taco salad
1 part diet Coke
1 part amaretto gelato

Not much to say about this one. It smells just like dog fart. It is great if you are self-conscious and own a dog.

Moderate volume
Moderate potency
Low shart risk

THE MAN FROM NANTUCKET

4 parts whole steamed crab (must eat *everything* but the shell)
2 parts potatoes
1 parts corn on the cob
1 part Coors Light
1 part warm apple pie

Smells like oysters boiled in sour milk. Has uncanny ability to slide past the anal sphincter without warning.

Low volume
High potency
High shart risk

THE TUSCAN

5 parts clam, shrimp, and squid pasta
2 parts lobster bisque
2 parts chocolate cake
1 part light beer
1 part coffee

Smells like combination of old leather and beached seaweed.

Moderate volume
Moderate potency
Low shart risk

EXIT THE DRAGON (A.K.A. THE FART OF WAR)

4 parts egg foo young with hot sauce
2 parts Yuengling light beer
1 part chips and salsa

Deep, complex odor that takes one off guard. Relentless—appears to know your next move before you make it. Gas remains even after a bowel movement. You can't get rid of it, you just have to wait it out.

High volume
High potency
Moderate shart risk

THE DUNKEL

6 parts Hofbräu Dunkel beer
2 parts fried pickles
2 parts fried sauerkraut and ham balls
2 parts potato pancakes

One of the bad actors on this list—very, very bad. Unsettling, putrid, rancid odor that sticks to everything. How could something that tastes so good come out smelling so bad? Frustrating longevity. You'll be yelling *Dunkel!* after every fart as a warning to your loved ones.

High volume
High potency
Moderate shart risk

THE LONE STAR

4 parts Texas Roadhouse T-bone steak
2 parts chili with cheese
2 parts green beans and bacon
2 parts Yuenling black and tan beer (tall)
1 part buttered bread

It's not hard to predict the ending of this story. Smells like a stockyard on a hot day. You won't be able to tolerate your own gas. Problem is, you can't run from yourself. Takes about six hours to run its course.

High volume
Moderate potency
Low shart risk

THE GREEN LANTERN

3 parts southwest chicken flatbread sandwich (Weight Watchers)
3 parts crunchy, baked green peas
1 part apple
1 part orange
1 part Coke Zero

Occurs after getting carried away nibbling on green pea snacks and finishing the entire package. Very potent, so don't take this one lightly. Cramp-inducing volume. Initially mimics early food-poisoning symptoms. Smells of compost and boiled chitterlings.

Outrageous volume
High potency
Moderate shart risk

SWAMP-ASS

6 parts seaweed soup (boiled water, seaweed-soup-mix
    packet, tofu, shrimp, bok choy, soy sauce, and Sriracha
    hot sauce)
3 parts Michelob Ultra Cactus Lime beer

A smell most consistent with warm swamp-water, with a
good measure of dead deer thrown in.

Low volume
High potency
Moderate shart risk

True story—I had the good fortune of riding with a
carload of women when I was stricken with a bad case of
swamp-ass. I also had the good fortune of owning a car
with a window lockout button at my disposal. After crap-
ping myself, I locked out all the windows in the car. Within

ten seconds I began receiving sharp criticisms, protests, and cutting remarks from all seating areas. During the ensuing melee, I overheard my sister-in-law launch into a short coughing spell, which was capped off with a loud dry heave. Now I have been pulling this kind of shit for a long time, but up to that point, I had never actually caused anyone to gag. I laughed until I cried. Success on such a colossal scale is hard to recover from, however. Why, you ask? Because how does one top such a feat? The only direction to go from there is down. It's almost depressing.

THE WOODSMAN

4 parts chicken quesadilla (with onions, green peppers, tomatoes, and cheese)
2 parts cherry wine
1 part milk

Dry with an unmistakable, earthy, rotting-wood bouquet. Employ this recipe when you want to get closer to nature.

Moderate volume
Moderate potency
Low shart risk

CAROLINA CLOGGER

4 parts Carolina-style chicken and pulled-pork barbecue
2 parts cole slaw
2 parts baked beans
1 part light beer
1 part FUO (fever of unknown origin)

The Clogger stands out from the crowd with a hard-hitting one-two punch of feces and BO. Strong notes of vinegar and poop predominate early, eventually giving way to lingering, spoiled-milk finish. Scent is highly complex.

Moderate volume
High potency
Low shart risk

BANKOK CHRISTMAS MIRACLE

3 parts red curry beef stew
3 parts smoked duck
2 parts micro brew
2 parts rice

Starts off with a faint peaty aroma, which complements its light, boiled-tendon entrance. Hints of smokiness then give way to a clean, dry finish.

Moderate volume
Low potency
Low shart risk

HOW BIZARRE, HOW BIZARRE

4 parts sirloin burger Campbell's Chunky soup
2 parts tangelos
2 parts stale Christmas shortbread cookies
1 part cheese

Smells a lot like sirloin burger and old cheese—except corrupted. Like Bizarro Superman: you recognize him, but something just ain't right. Wife anger factor very high due to worse-than-average odor and longevity.

High volume
Moderate to high potency
Low shart risk

Tip: Excellent choice for the Surprise

ENEMY MINE

4 parts Nacho Cheese Doritos
3 parts grilled cheese sandwich
3 parts tomato bisque soup
1 part Sam Adam's Black Lager

Very deep, heavy, arresting gas. It will hold an entire room hostage for twenty minutes. One of the few recipes on the list that can backfire on you. Angering and long-lasting. No escape, because no matter where you go, there you are.

Moderate volume
Outrageous potency
Moderate shart risk

MOVIE THEATER MESS

4 parts hamburger with the works
1 bottle hard cider
1 entire box of Dots
1/2 box of Whoppers

Smells like moldy sourdough bread that's been soaked in urine and allowed to sit in a hot car.

High volume
Moderate potency
Low shart risk

WHAT THE KALE?

4 parts baked kale with seasoned salt
2 parts Tater Tots and ketchup
1 part orange juice

Smells like steamed carrots and vomit (after eating at Long John Silver's).

Moderate volume
Moderate to high potency
Low shart risk

THE NIGHT STALKER

5 parts braised lamb chops
3 parts mashed potatoes
2 parts cooked broccoli
3 parts rhubarb cheesecake
1 part red wine

This recipe takes four to five hours to fully develop. If eaten at dinner, you will go to bed oblivious of the danger lurking in your gut. Apparently odor is comparable to a New York sewer (see below).

Impressive volume and longevity
Moderate potency
Low shart risk

True story—I listed this one after my wife brought it to my attention. She claims that one night my gas was so potent she incorporated it into her dream. In this dream she is trapped in a New York sewer. No matter where she went or how far she ran, she could not find a way out. Upon waking she quickly identified the source of her torment. She had been the victim of a savage dutch-oven-style bedroom attack. I was still asleep, so I am relying on her account to describe the scene: "It came in waves. I would just recover from one when another would arrive. It smelled like a New York sewer on the day after Thanksgiving." She didn't know how long the ordeal lasted, but she was exhausted the following day.

CHILI RE-DEAUX

6 parts chili (multiple bowls over a two-day period)
1 part beer or diet cola
1 part tortilla chips
1 part shredded cheese
1 part sour cream

Smells like a combination of deviled eggs, old uncooked hamburger, and smoked paprika. That is as accurate as I can get.

High volume and excellent longevity
Moderate potency
Low shart risk

LOW-HANGING FRUIT (A.K.A. GREEK TRAGEDY)

4 parts moussaka
2 parts Vegemite with greek yogurt
2 parts greek rice
1 part greek coffee

Sickly sweet and sour at the same time. In short, it smells like old men's balls. How do I know what old men's balls smell like? Well, I dont. I am guessing that everyon's balls smell fiendishly alike. I then assume, maybe incorrectly, that once balls get to a certain age they just smell worse.

Moderate volume with excellent longevity
Extreme potency
Moderate shart risk

GRIM REAPER

6 parts smoked ribs
3 parts baked beans
1 part original potato chips
1 part dill pickles
1 part 2% milk

This one takes a while to develop. You can feel it moving through your colon. You know it's coming and fear its arrival. Like death, however, there is nothing you can do to stop it. Creates a deep, rich aroma that will linger in whatever space you occupy for at least ten minutes. Reminiscent of old blood, dirty socks, and heavy equipment.

Low volume
Very high potency
Moderate shart risk

THE RIDDLER

4 parts sloppy joe
2 parts cooked asparagus
1 part cold milk

Requires eight hours of incubation and a fresh shower. Smells like soap and post-workout butt in the same moment. It's rather confusing.

Low volume
Moderate potency
Low shart risk

SLUMDOG MILLIONAIRE

5 parts murgh makani (butter chicken)
3 parts palak paneer (spinach in cream sauce)
2 parts Raita (indian yogurt salad)
2 parts spicy chutney on nan bread
1 part Kingfisher beer

Sacred Hindu cow dung predominates early. This eventually gives way to notes of curry, black mustard, turmeric, and coriander in a background of aged cheese. It's what I imagine washing clothes in the sewers of Delhi would smell like.

Moderate volume
High potency
High shart risk

KALASHNIKOV

4 parts meatloaf (any type will do)
3 parts baked beans in BBQ sauce
2 parts mashed potatoes
2 bottles Killian's Irish Red beer

Like an AK-47, this is a surprisingly simple combination that is reliable and flat-out deadly. It smells like turd to the tenth power. I have induced a gag reflex in my eighteen-year-old nephew during a fart duel (In case anyone is keeping score, that's the second time I have made someone gag).

Moderate volume
High potency
Low shart risk

BERKLEY THAI TEMPLE OF DOOM

2 parts beef curry (panang)
2 parts chicken and cashews
2 parts spicy pho with beef balls
1 part mangos with sweet sticky rice
1 part thai tea
1 part heavy dose of feet and armpit funk from multiple Berkley "wippies"

Steamy, wet, and hot—like the jungles of Thailand. Overall odor is underwhelming and forgettable. You should do this one mostly for the dining experience.

Low volume
Moderate potency
high shart risk

TIP: "Wippies" are wannabe hippies who require a continuous cash infusion from their wealthy families to maintain a high standard of living while they rebel against capitalism and basic hygiene.

Angus Beeftickle MD

CODE RED

4 parts strawberry Twizzlers (entire 1 lb bag)
2 parts stuffed green pepper
1 part Coke Zero

High volume that quickly pressurizes in your rectum. Difficult to hold back at times. Pungent, mossy background with notes of blue cheese.

High volume
Moderate potency
Low shart risk

SONIC BOOM

4 parts Chicago-style hot dogs
1 parts Tater Tots
1 part chocolate malt

Odor is reminiscent of fried baloney and dog's feet.

Moderate volume
Moderate potency
Low shart risk

FISH BANQUET

4 parts Orange Roughy
2 parts cauliflower
1 part chocolate bridge mix
1 part Coors Banquet beer

A "banquet" of odors assault your olfactory nerve simulta-neously. Best described as combination of meat-juice (slimy liquid that spills out of ground beef package on to your refrigerator shelf), generic turd, and uncleaned fish tank.

Moderate to high volume
Moderate potency
Low shart risk

BIGFOOT'S DICK

4 parts chicken fried steak with cream gravy
2 parts collard greens with hot sauce
2 parts black eyed peas
1 part cheesecake
1 part wheat beer

If you have ever longed to know what Bigfoot's dick smells like but didn't want to risk your life to find out, this recipe is for you. Smell reminds me of a combination of rotten cheese, dried poop, and buck scent (A not-so-subtle liquid used to bait deer. Smells similar to dog's butt glands).

Moderate volume with with surprising longevity
High potency
Moderate shart risk

WARNING

M any of these recipes—hell, all of 'em—are based on my narrow and often nutritionally deficient diet. I must insist that readers do not attempt to re-create this diet on a routine basis. And if you are thinking to yourself, "Most of these recipes involve beer," you'd be right. The best ones definitely do.

❖ ❖ ❖

CHAPTER VI

COMMITMENT

OK, so you have a vague recollection of the past several chapters. You have a loose grasp of the subject matter. Now you think you understand what it takes to break the shackles of Colonic Restraint. Don't get cocky. If you really want to know what it's all about, then you have to commit. You have to fart in public.

Believe me, it's not easy. The first public fart is very difficult, but you can't walk a mile without taking the first step. My challenge to you is simple. You must stop contemplating and start doing. You must be a stinker and not a thinker. I know you are ready; I can smell these things.

A few suggestions to get sharted—er, started. The beginner should start with close friends and family. Practice "The Mad Hatter" on your wife while you're driving. Use "The Surprise" on your children and neighbors. Rip stupid while your friend is in his backswing. Once you have built up some confidence, move on to coworkers and clergy. You will find this a difficult transition, as these people are usually less forgiving.

I suggest starting with a silent Smooth Criminal in and around a bank of cubicles. Keep walking, lest you want to be exposed. Once your care factor is low enough, lay a truck-full of ass in your own cubicle just before a coworker is due with some documents; your office mate damn sure will know what was done and who done it. If you can still hold your chin up, you have made a major breakthrough.

I have found that starting with silent farts is easier than audible ones—even around strangers. It takes a while before one is truly ready to fart *loudly* in public. For your first attempt, try a location where anonymity is still a possibility. The movie theater is a great place to bust your cherry. Wait until the movie is about to start, when it is dark and quiet. Theaters usually have great acoustics, so dozens of people will be within earshot. Trust me, this one always gets a laugh. Number one, no one sees it coming. Number two, people going to the movies are usually in an upbeat, relaxed mood. The outburst ultimately adds to the experience, as most of the moviegoers will talk more about the huge fart somebody let than they will the movie.

The library is a great next step. Pick a table that is surrounded by bookshelves and out of the way. This will provide you with a sense of security. There is some technique to library farts, as you can use the wooden chairs as a backboard to amplify the sound. You won't get it right at first, but keep at it. A great fart recipe for this venue is the Power Lifter, as it provides great volume, low shart risk, and a pleasant odor.

Once you cross this threshold, there is no going back. You will start to shed your insecurities, and a bold new you will emerge. You will worry less about what others think and focus more on personal satisfaction. Obstacles in other areas of your life will tend to seem smaller: If I can do this, what other challenges can I rise to? It is much like the feeling one gets after running a marathon or eating an entire Butterballl turkey by oneself.

If you are still reading and have not yet completed the challenge, stop. This message is not intended for you. You have proven nothing and remain as part of the problem. For those of you who have completed the challenge, welcome. Welcome into the brotherhood of the resistance. You are now part of the solution and must share your knowledge and skill with others. This is the burden we must bear.

There are no freeloaders here. If you wish to remain in good standing, you must contribute. As part of your initiation ceremony, you must log on to your favorite social media medium and share some of your most memorable fart stories with the world. Fear not, for we are all in the trust tree together. No one will be singled out, as everybody receives equal ridicule here. You will also be expected to contribute at least one fart recipe to our growing collection. Please don't include any personal information. No one gives a shit, anyway.

Well, it appears my work here is done. Honestly, I don't know whether to slap you or kiss you. I am proud of you, on some level, but I have also lost all respect for what you have allowed yourself to become.

Oh, by the way. If you thought I was going to tell you my name, you're dumber than I thought. By remaining anonymous, I can continue to roam the countryside doing thankless, unnecessary work without losing my job.

❖ ❖ ❖

References

1. K. R. Price, Jenny Lewis, G. M. Wyatt, and G. R. Fenwick. Flatulence - Causes, relation to diet and remedies. Die Nahrung: 32 (1988) 6, 609-626.

2. Edwin L. Murphy, Heide Horsley, and Horace K. Burr. Fractionation of dry bean extracts which increase carbon dioxide egestion in human flatus. Journal of Agricultural and Food Chemistry: 20 (1972) 813-817.

3. Tomlin, J., Lowis, C., Read, N. W. Investigation of normal flatus production in healthy volunteers. Gut: 32 (1991) 665-669.